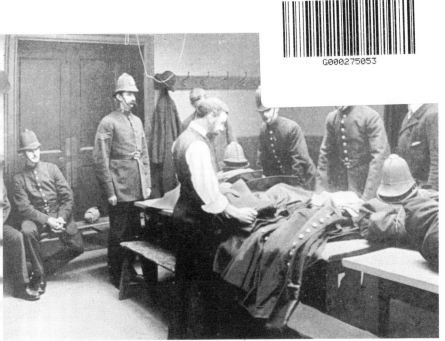

A late nineteenth-century clothing parade with the sergeant bringing a party of recruits to the force tailor to be fitted with their uniform. Which force they belong to is not known but before making new uniform attempts would be made to equip the new men with old, possibly used stock. Otherwise each uniform was made to measure.

POLICE UNIFORM AND EQUIPMENT

A. A. Clarke

Shire Publications Ltd

CONTENTS

Printed in Great Britain by C. I. Thomas & Sons (Haverfordwest) Ltd, Press Buildings, Merlins Bridge, Haverfordwest, Dyfed SA61 1XF.

British Library Cataloguing in Publication Data: Clarke, A. A. Police uniform and equipment. 1. Great Britain. Police, history. I. Title. 363.20941. ISBN 0-7478-0126-6.

ACKNOWLEDGEMENTS

I would like to acknowledge my debt to many organisations and individuals who have assisted in the preparation of this Album, and in particular the Librarian of the Police Staff College, curators of museums in York, Hull and Carlisle, of the Victoria and Albert Museum in London and of the Metropolitan Police Museum Store, and officers of the Police Insignia Collectors' Society.

Illustrations are acknowledged to the following, who either supplied photographs or allowed me to photograph exhibits in their possession: Chief Constable of Avon and Somerset, pages 6 (bottom) and 9; R. Brewster Esquire, page 20 (middle row, left and centre); Commissioner, City of London, page 19 (top left); Chief Constable of Devon and Cornwall, page 6 (top left); Douglas Elliott, page 13 (top); S. D. Gall, Esquire, page 27 (top); Chief Constable of Gloucestershire, page 23 (top right); Hull Daily Mail, page 5 (left); Chief Constable of Humberside, pages 1, 7, 12 (top right), 17 (top left), 18 (bottom), 24 (bottom), 28 (right) and 29 (top); Chief Constable of Kent, pages 3, 13 (bottom) and 16 (top); Chief Constable of Lincolnshire, page 20 (second row from top); Chief Constable of Greater Manchester, pages 8 (top), 11 (bottom) and 16 (bottom); Commissioner of the Metropolitan Police, pages 8 (bottom), 10 (top left), 15 (top), 24 (top left and right), 29 (bottom) and 30; Chief Constable of North Yorkshire, pages 2 and 25; Pompadour Gallery and Bryan Fosten, page 18 (top); Ripon Police and Prison Museum, pages 10 (bottom), 11 (top) and 14 (left); Chief Constable of South Wales, pages 5 (right) and 19 (top right); Chief Constable of Sussex, pages 17 (bottom) and 23 (top left); Chief Constable of Thames Valley, pages 15 (middle) and 26 (bottom); A. D. Tunstall Esquire, page 6 (top right); Chief Constable of West Mercia, page 17 (top centre and right); Chief Constable of West Yorkshire, pages 14 (right) and 22 (right); Sergeant Norman Woollons, pages 12 (top left, middle and bottom), 15 (bottom), 20 (top, centre right and bottom), 21, 23 (bottom), 26 (top) and 27 (bottom); ex-Sergeant Clive Widd, page 22 (left).

Above right: *Caricature of a late eighteenth-century watchman drawn by the celebrated cartoonist Thomas Rowlandson and presented by Lord Cathcart to the Chief Constable of the North Riding of Yorkshire in 1866.*

Cover: *An oil painting of Constable 101 of Kingston upon Hull (c.1840). He is dressed in typical winter uniform of the time — top hat, blue swallow-tailed coat and matching trousers. The artist is unknown.*

The complete borough police force of Tenterden, Kent, just before the start of the amalgamation of such tiny units into their surrounding counties in 1898.

INTRODUCTION

Before the introduction of 'Bobbies' by the Home Secretary, Robert Peel, in 1829, and except when military force was used to quell public disorder, a system of law enforcement had developed in England and Wales based on its citizens policing themselves. Since at least Norman times communities had elected a constable annually as one of their important officers and from 1285 the inhabitants took turns as watchmen to guard the walls and gates of their towns from sunset to sunrise daily.

The system lasted for over five hundred years but gradually the practice grew of wealthier citizens paying deputies when it was their turn to be parish constable and towns started to use paid watchmen. Both jobs increasingly became permanent employment for men of very low ability. The pay was poor and their status low. By the eighteenth century a motley array of parish constables, watchmen and petty officials was having little effect on the growing problem, in an expanding population, of crime and disorder, particularly in London and other towns. Despite the gradual widening of watchmen's duties to patrol larger parts of towns the system was inefficient and corruption rife. There was also great resistance to reform and particularly to the introduction of organised police forces because it was feared it would cause loss of individual liberty through greater central control.

In 1748 Henry Fielding, the novelist, was appointed Chief Magistrate at Bow Street in London. He saw the need to follow other European countries and to introduce paid and uniformed police forces. In 1750 he formed a small permanent group of constables, which evolved into the famous Bow Street Runners. When he died in 1754, his

3

brother John succeeded him as Chief Magistrate and in 1763 he introduced the first horse patrol of eight men to combat highwaymen on approach roads to London. Operating only at night, they were soon disbanded owing to lack of finance.

By 1797 Henry Fielding's Bow Street Runners had expanded to some 68 men and in 1798 a force of sixty salaried constables was appointed as the Thames Marine River Police to combat an estimated ten thousand thieves, footpads and prostitutes in London's dockland. Originally paid for by West India merchants, it was so successful that the Thames River Police Act of 1800 converted it to a public body. They did not wear uniform.

Despite these efforts the eighteenth century ended with little improvement in crime and disorder. Watchmen or bellmen still shuffled through ill lit streets in towns at night. Dressed in long capes or gowns and carrying staves and dim lanterns, they called out the time and weather, so revealing themselves to wrongdoers and inviting pranks. Any significant outbreak of public disorder required deployment of the military, who had a reputation for being extremely harsh.

In 1805 Sir John Ford revived John Fielding's idea and formed a sixty-strong horse patrol on roads within 20 miles (32 km) of London. Known as the Bow Street Mounted Horse Patrol, it worked at night and in 1821 was reinforced by a hundred-strong second echelon curiously known as the Unmounted Horse Patrol. The three bodies, Runners, Mounted and Unmounted horse patrols, were controlled, as their name suggests, from Bow Street Magistrates' Court in London.

The Mounted Patrol was the first uniformed police unit in England and Wales. They wore blue greatcoats with yellow metal buttons, scarlet waistcoats, blue trousers, wellington boots, white gloves and black leather top hats. From the waistcoats came the nickname 'Robin Redbreasts'. Their unmounted colleagues were given no uniform but were issued with truncheons, cutlasses and occasionally pistols.

The last Bow Street Patrol to be introduced was by Robert Peel himself, when,

as Home Secretary in 1822, he formed the first foot patrol for working by day. The 27 men of this unit were mostly ex-soldier and Peel felt 'they would be proud of their establishment if they were dressed as their mounted colleagues'.

Still not satisfied and concentrating on London, Peel overcame considerable opposition and on 19th July 1829 his bill for 'Improving the Police in and around the Metropolis' became law. He quickly set about establishing comprehensive policing for the capital. Colonel Rowan, late of the Army and Royal Irish Constabulary, and Richard Mayne, a young barrister, were appointed co-commissioners and found accommodation at 4 Whitehall Place, which backed on to a narrow lane known as Scotland Yard. The legislation gave wide discretion in organising London's new Metropolitan Police and Rowan and Mayne formed seventeen police divisions with newly named superintendents in charge. Ranks of inspector and sergeant were created, titles taken from the Bow Street Patrols and army respectively, and, together with traditionally named constables, the force totalled nearly three thousand men.

Their aim was to establish an organisation whose members could relate to ordinary citizens. Recruitment of gentlemen and officers of the Army was discouraged and many initial supervisory officers had been senior non-commissioned officers in the forces. Some existing parish constables and watchmen were recruited but most of the new force were ordinary citizens — tradesmen, farmworkers and labourers.

Observing the benefits of the new London force, progressive towns like Liverpool and Bristol carried out some reorganisation of their own police in following years but elsewhere things remained unchanged.

It was not until 1835 that by the Municipal Corporations Act 178 boroughs were allowed to form watch committees of their town councils with responsibility for establishing new-style police forces. Some accepted the challenge immediately but by 1837 only half had created proper forces and thirty had still made no progress by 1845. Individual acts were necessary to

Left: *Reconstruction of the uniforms of early police in Kingston upon Hull with uniforms meticulously copied from old patterns. An inspector is shown on the right in a frock-coat and the constable on the left has a blue swallow-tailed tunic over white summer-weight trousers. Identification is embroidered on the collars and both men wear glazed top hats. Only the stocks are missing.*

Right: *An early photograph taken about 1854-6 of Constable 3 William Wallbridge, Cardiff police, wearing summer uniform including a belt with snake fastening. Forces began to change to a more modern style of uniform soon after this time.*

deal with some large but unchartered towns such as Manchester and Birmingham.

Worried by Chartist movement riots, the government looked at policing rural areas and in 1839 a County Police Act empowered but did not require formation of new police forces in the shires. Considerable resistance was forthcoming from all-powerful magistrates in some counties and, while Essex, Lancashire and a few others acted quickly, it was not until a mandatory Police Act of 1856 that all counties introduced new-style forces. When forming their forces, many counties followed a growing trend of appointing ex-Army officers as chief constables. The practice was continued until the second half of the twentieth century.

During the late nineteenth century there began a trend to reorganise and amalgamate forces which resulted in the number of police forces in England and Wales being reduced from a maximum of 231 in 1888 to an eventual 43 in 1990.

5

Above left: *A constable in the Devonshire Constabulary c.1900 wearing a slouch or bush hat, which was issued by that force and only one other in England and Wales — Monmouthshire. It was introduced by ex-military chief constables who had seen service in the South Africa police. The tunic has two breast pockets and can be seen to be of a very coarse type of material.*

Above right: *The Chief Constable of Newcastle-under-Lyme, Staffordshire, from 1903 to 1913, showing the pillbox-style forage cap braided and with silver lace braid on the peak denoting senior rank. Heavy and generous knotting and braiding on the tunic made it an expensive item to make.*

Left: *A sergeant, two inspectors and a superintendent (in the background) of Reading Borough police about 1890, showing the pillbox-style forage caps of senior officers with the heavily braided tunics which were identical for inspectors and superintendents.*

A possibly unique photograph of Edwardian tailors preparing uniforms for the borough police in Grimsby. The tunics in view were mainly for sergeants and show an unusual crown between the rank chevrons and first-aid badges. This was probably just a decorative addition.

DEVELOPMENT OF THE UNIFORM

Although initially indifferent to the dress of his London police, Peel soon realised it was a matter of some importance. It was originally envisaged that they would appear in blue and scarlet, based, no doubt, on the uniform of the Bow Street Patrols, but such was the resistance to the formation of a new police force, and particularly to anything with military connotations, that many felt they should not wear uniform. The question was probably settled by the attitude of Colonel Rowan, who argued that uniform was essential to foster an *esprit de corps.*

The compromise was for a non-military uniform. Identical sets of clothing were issued which, while they could have been worn by any man in the street, were not far removed from the uniform of the Bow Street Patrols or the dress uniform of a naval bosun. As one shrewd observer remarked, 'The hat was probably just homely enough to save the day.'

This was a dark-coloured civilian-style top hat also known as a 'stovepipe' and described as having 'A black leather top with 1/2 inch (13 mm) overlap onto a black beaver crown, 6 inches (152 mm) tall with reinforced side stays of cane on either side, 7 inches (178 mm) wide; 7 1/2 inches (191 mm) front to back. Black braid round base ... 2 inches (51 mm) wide brim piped with black braid.' It was heavy to wear but said to have been designed not only to protect the wearer but also to act as a convenient step when scaling walls in pursuit of criminals.

As additional protection, a 4 inch (102 mm) high leather stock was worn round the neck to prevent garrotting, or strangulation by a piece of cord. It was reduced to 2 inches (51 mm) high in 1845.

The blue swallow-tailed frock-coat had seven gilt buttons down the front which were stamped with the crown and the ini-

7

A parade of top-hatted Manchester police about 1860 showing the change in uniform style. Gone were the cut-away swallow tails, replaced by a full-skirted, almost knee-length garment.

tials MP. The wearer's divisional letter and number were embroidered in white on the raised collar.

Blue trousers were issued for winter wear and lighter white ones for the summer, with wellington boots as footwear. Rather incongruously, but no doubt befitting their civilian image, early police in the provinces were permitted to carry umbrellas on duty, a practice which continued in some parts until the middle of the century.

Oilskin capes were provided for wet weather and, apart from a change of material to a heavy melton cloth, remained standard issue until the 1970s. Overcoats, originally brown in colour, were supplied for the winter and the uniform was completed by a pair of white gloves.

Policemen were instructed to wear uniform at all times except when in bed. After complaints about policemen in uniform gossiping, blue and white striped armbands were issued in 1830, to be worn on the left sleeve of men on duty. Generally the stripes on the armband were vertical but a few forces used horizontally striped armbands.

The vertically striped duty armband worn usually on the left sleeve of the tunic to distinguish men who were actually on duty. Such indication had become necessary as policemen were required to wear uniform at all times whether on or off duty.

Confusingly, before the use of French-style chevrons, worn by the British army since 1802, some police forces denoted sergeant rank by horizontally striped armbands worn on the right sleeve, variously either above or below the elbow. The separate City of London force wore red and white armbands.

Not until the end of the nineteenth century did some forces allow their men to wear civilian clothes when off duty and 'duty' armbands were not withdrawn in the Metropolitan Police until 1968.

Most early police forces required men to pay a deposit for their uniform. The West Riding of Yorkshire took 5 shillings and returned it when the uniform was handed in, provided it was in good condition. If a man resigned within six months of joining, 2 shillings were deducted from his deposit to pay for altering the uniform to fit his successor. The watch committee of York directed that constables should mend their own uniforms unless the chief constable ordered otherwise.

Despite the efforts of Peel and the first commissioners to make the new police acceptable to the public, hostility led to many nicknames being coined, often related to the uniform. In addition to 'Bobbies' and 'Peelers', directed at the founder himself, names such as 'the Blue Army', 'Blue Locusts' and 'Raw Lobsters' proliferated. Children in the streets recited the rhyme:

'There goes a bobby in his black shiny hat
And his belly full of fat.'

New forces in the provinces generally found it expedient and financially prudent to adopt uniform already tried and tested in London. Having first obtained samples from a supplier to the London force such as Charles Hibbert of Holborn, officials would often choose a local, cheaper manufacturer to clothe their own men. Sometimes this search for economy resulted in difficulties and delays and the Hull force had to start with second-hand capes.

A desire to secure and retain local individuality resulted in some early forces, including those of the West Riding, Lancashire, Derbyshire and Montgomeryshire, ordering green instead of blue uniforms. Wigan chose brown while Dorset clothed its men in light grey but they withdrew them after pressure from the Home Office. Eventually dark blue prevailed, perhaps because dirt was more easily concealed. Certainly soot from the oil lamps carried

Inspector Newport and Chief Inspector Noble of Bath Borough police photographed after arresting two violent murderers in 1896. Their tunics are comparatively plain and the heavy braiding so favoured by many forces is missing, thus making the garments much cheaper.

on their belts could badly stain tunics.

In the early 1900s at least two forces, Devon and Monmouthshire, issued unusual bush hats for general duty. Climate and the work soon proved their unsuitability and they were discontinued. In 1910 Monmouthshire's neighbour, Newport Borough, strongly resisted the issue of white helmets and a seventy-strong petition from constables resulted in the proposal being withdrawn.

The style and material of the uniforms of constables and sergeants were generally similar except that sergeants, from the 1860s, had silver-plated rather than cloth-covered cuff buttons, mohair collars and silver lace arm chevrons to distinguish their rank. Higher ranks were denoted not so much by badges as by the quality of the uniform. In 1830 a Kentish constable's complete uniform cost £4 6s 3d with one shilling extra for a sergeant's mohair collar. The superintendent's frock-coat alone, heavily braided and with silver lace on collar and cuffs, cost £6 5s 0d.

An extract from a Lancashire Constabulary memorandum at the beginning of the twentieth century sets out the requirements for an inspector's frock-coat:

'The collar is to be of a correct stand-up shape, not sloping, 1½ inches [38 mm] deep all round and to fasten with a hook at the top and bottom. The braid trimming is to be as follows; — Half inch [13 mm] braid is to be laid flat down front edge of each side of coat. Tracing braid to be laid next, this at an interval of a quarter of an inch [6 mm] and carried round the collar seam. Inch [25 mm] braid round each cuff, bottom edges on underside, two inches [51 mm] from and parallel with the edge of the cuff and on the top side, carried upwards to a neat point 6½ inches [165 mm] from the end of the cuff. Inch [25 mm] braid to be laid along the edges of the pleats on each skirt at the back with a rose curving inwards at the top, one half above waist seam, and a rose curving outwards at the bottom. The length including roses to be 12 inches [305 mm]. An olivette to be fixed to the centre of each rose, the upwards points turned outwards at an angle of 45 degrees.'

Left: *Most chief constables had ceremonial dress uniform for special occasions and wore civilian clothes for everyday duty. No standard pattern was laid down and designs were individual but usually styled on military or diplomatic dress. The resplendent tunic of Sir Edward Bradford, Commissioner of the Metropolitan Police 1890-1903, is a splendid example of the very best.*

Below: *The one ceremonial helmet in Scarborough belonged to the chief constable in the early 1900s. Typically decorated with impressive helmet badge or plate on front, it has an ornate ball-style ventilator piece on top, to which is fixed a heavy military-style helmet chain for extra decoration.*

Above: *Captain L. A. Lindsay, Chief Constable of Glamorgan, c.1920, wears a heavily chained ceremonial helmet and has embellished his tunic with a highly polished Sam Browne belt, to which has been fixed a duplicate of his helmet badge or plate together with a heavily chained police whistle.*

Frock-coats for senior ranks were discontinued before the First World War but braid continued, albeit to a lesser degree, on tunics and trousers.

Before government-inspired standardisation in the twentieth century, changes in police uniform were haphazard and depended on local preference. It is ironic that a public which thirty years previously had steadfastly resisted a military-like force was, by the 1860s, calling for military efficiency in the police. Policemen were becoming an accepted and welcome part of everyday life and, with more ex-soldiers being recruited as chief constables, an almost inevitable connection grew between the uniforms of police and soldiers. The British Army was copying aspects of first French and then German uniforms and this became reflected in the style of police dress.

Top hats tended to look shabby; the leather tops cracked and gave policemen

John Holdgate, the long-serving Chief Constable of Bolton (1877-1911), chose a frock-coat with extensive and dramatic braiding on the shoulders and lower sleeves only.

An 1890 Scarborough policeman still wearing the curly-brim style helmet. His armband is fixed to his left sleeve indicating he is on duty and the lamp fixed in front of the lamp guard indicates he is on night duty. The buttons on his greatcoat are simple everyday bone buttons as on civilian clothing.

headaches. Coincidentally during the late 1850s and early 1860s they went out of fashion in civilian life and the Army began to wear helmets. Originally introduced by the Russians, helmets had been taken up by the increasingly powerful Prussian army. From 1863 the Metropolitan Police began issuing similar helmets made of cloth-covered cork and the traditional British police helmet was born.

The first helmets had a raised spine running from the top down the back and were known as 'combed'. They had unusually flat, slightly curled brims, similar to a bowler hat. Quite soon this brim became simpler and more like the present style, and many forces removed the comb.

Left: *A white general-duty helmet issued by a few forces for summer wear. This model is an early six-panelled version issued by Salford Borough in the late nineteenth or early twentieth century.*

Right: *The interior webbing support of a 1980s specially reinforced helmet for wear during situations when public order may break down. This headgear was eventually replaced by the NATO riot helmet.*

Variations in helmet style were widespread, many forces adopting highly decorative versions with shiny chain chinstraps and elaborate ventilator pieces in the form of spikes, globes or rosettes on top for ceremonial duties. Some, like Worcester City, took such helmets into general use. A few purchased just one for the chief constable.

A variety of material was used to construct helmets, including plaited straw versions in Luton, Salisbury and elsewhere for summer wear. The straw was covered with blue cloth in Manchester but uncovered in Luton and Salisbury. Modern helmets are constructed mainly of compressed cork and covered either with specially treated rabbit skin or good-quality melton cloth.

Left: *Three variations in decoration on modern police helmets, c.1953-67. (Left to right) Grimsby Borough, with ornate ventilator piece and side rose; Lincolnshire County, with simpler ventilator piece but with silver band; Leicester and Rutland, with a rose in place of the silver band.*

Right: *Different helmet shapes, 1953-67. (Left to right) Berkshire, plain and unadorned except for a chrome ventilator rose; the squat 1970s-style reinforced motorcycle helmet, from Lincolnshire; an East Riding of Yorkshire combed helmet.*

While some forces, particularly in urban areas, took helmets as standard headgear, many counties wore French-style pillbox forage caps for normal daily duties but had helmets issued for special or ceremonial occasions. Superintendents, inspectors and office staff all wore the pillbox caps well into the twentieth century. Cheshire and Kent were unusual, the former adopting a shako-style hat while Kent policemen wore

Right: Constable T. J. Phillips (1920-1) in Cheshire's neighbouring county of Shropshire, wearing his county's slightly shorter version of the Cheshire shako. He wears the first-aid badge on the right arm and he has two Boer War campaign medals.

Below: A section of Sevenoaks division of Kent police in 1893 wearing their kepis. The two chevrons worn by two of the men indicate they are senior constables on top rate of pay. The star on the sleeve of the one seated on the right is a merit star probably indicating he was qualified for promotion.

13

Left: *A late nineteenth-century photograph of a Leeds City constable wearing a knee-length wide-skirted tunic with first-aid badge on the right arm. The helmet has an unusual appearance with a japanned peak and band.*

Right: *A constable of the West Riding of Yorkshire before 1914, wearing the close-fitting Grenadier Guards style tunic of the time, completely plain and reaching just below the hips. The Yorkshire rose accompanies his collar numerals.*

Left: *A typical police leather night-duty belt with cheap 'snake' form of buckle and with lamp guard attached to prevent oil from lamps damaging uniform cloth. Belts were not withdrawn in most forces until around the 1960s.*

Right: *A belt from Reading Borough police force showing a more decorative fastening with Victorian crown.*

a kepi, both styles copied from the French. Force referendums, held to decide which form of headgear to use, were nearly always in favour of the helmet.

With changes in headgear came a new style of tunic. The long garments held water and caused rheumatism in the knees, and the swallow tails were replaced by looser garments reaching to between hip and knees, the precise length varying from force to force. They were closed at the neck and had seven or eight buttons down the front. The pockets were still concealed behind a rear vent. This opening was sometimes embellished with buttons as on the Grenadier Guards tunic, on which the London police tunic was based.

By the end of the nineteenth century the duty helmets were becoming simpler and more like the style recognised today. Tunics were generally shortened and provided with two breast pockets. Certain local oddities remained, as the following extract from the orders of East Riding police in the 1920s reveals:

'Sergeants and constables, when proceeding on duty per bicycle, during the daytime, must be dressed in proper cycling kit, viz. forage caps, serge jackets, cycling knickers, blue stockings and low shoes'.

Concern that care should be taken of uniform is highlighted in the same autumn order, when it instructs:

'The new serge jackets must be well brushed and carefully folded and put away for wear next Spring.'

The search for economy was particularly noticeable in smaller borough forces and, when wealthier neighbours advertised used uniform for disposal, towns such as Neath and Merthyr Tydfil were known to buy it for reissue to their own men!

The wearing of leather belts declined in the 1930s except for ceremonial or night duties but it was not until the 1960s that they were finally dispensed with at nights.

Differences in quality and style of uniform in forces resulted in the 1934 Dixon Committee addressing the problem of uniform standardisation. While justifying

Belt buckles from Halifax, Rutland and Oldham forces showing different decoration. The items are highly prized by collectors of police memorabilia.

15

The Kent pedal-cycle patrol about 1910 with similar uniform to the Manchester patrol shown below but with unusual side forage caps.

some local variations, it concluded that all police should 'be capable of turning out, in both garments and headdress, approximating closely enough to a uniform pattern as respects material and style'. The Committee felt this particularly necessary for cases where forces were called upon to aid one another.

They produced meticulously detailed specifications for a standard uniform, which was strongly supported by the Home Office. Since then the number of police forces has been drastically reduced, yet the preamble to another official committee on uniform which sat over fifty years after Dixon stated: 'The group was formed ... to consider whether there would be merit in seeking some degree of standardisation in the style and appearance of police officers in uniform.'

Rapid changes had been occurring in at-

titudes to clothes and uniform, particularly in the armed services. In the late 1940s there was much discussion on altering the tunic to an open-necked style. Official resistance was great but policemen voted overwhelmingly in support of the change. Initially it was agreed that open-necked tunics could be worn in the summer months as an experiment, but popular demand soon ensured they became standard wear.

During the 1960s, 1970s and 1980s a great variety of clothing styles were used by police. Increased mechanisation proved that helmets, overcoats and capes were cumbersome in vehicles. The adoption by the military of more casual operational uniform also influenced police thinking. The traditional helmet or cap and tunic still survived for basic outdoor foot and cycle patrol, although a high-quality tunic, based on that issued to army officers and orig-

Members of the Edwardian-style pedal-cycle patrol of the Manchester police with pillbox forage caps, normal tunics, cycling knickers or breeches and puttee-type leggings extending over the boots.

Above left: *After the Second World War the police dress rules, previously rigid, began to relax. This 1947 photograph shows the first policeman in Beverley, Humberside, allowed to remove his tunic in hot weather. His trousers, normally requiring braces, are secured with a borrowed Army webbing belt.*

Above centre: *A typical late 1980s policeman in working uniform in West Mercia with helmet and open-necked tunic with four built-in pockets. This tunic reaches just below the hip. Badges showing the force crest are fitted to the tunic lapels.*

Above right: *A development of the 1980s — an inspector in West Mercia wearing his normal working dress including a navy-blue heavy-duty NATO sweater with epaulettes bearing his rank insignia. The sweaters are more comfortable and less restrictive than tunics but their introduction is strenuously resisted by some chief constables.*

Right: *The early police motorcyclist. Constable Jack Phillpot of East Sussex on his 1930s BSA and dressed in soft cap, goggles, police tunic, gauntlets, breeches and leather gaiters.*

One of a series of paintings by Bryan Fosten of a London policeman in steel helmet and rubber boots and carrying a gas mask during the London Blitz, 1941.

material widely used. Ultimately some forces, following military example, issued heavy-duty navy-blue NATO sweaters for everyday use. Many chief constables still resolutely resisted such fundamental change but in forces such as West Mercia pullovers have been accepted as a smart and more comfortable alternative to the somewhat restrictive tunic.

Although used only occasionally, two types of uniform are worn by police in special situations. To operate effectively, officers required to use firearms need complete freedom of movement and, while not standing out as targets themselves, must be readily identifiable as police officers. Blue boiler suits and berets, with the word PO-LICE and a diced armband, provide the usual answer. In the second half of the twentieth century we have also seen the sad sight of British police in full riot gear, flameproof suit, heavy boots, helmet and visor and plastic shield, possibly leaving only one thing remaining from the original uniform provided for Peel's 'bobbies' — the colour blue!

Unusual and little remembered facets of police work involved firefighting and removing the sick to hospital. An act of 1774 required each parish to keep a fire appliance and police were the obvious source of manpower. Until the outbreak of the Second World War most forces staffed local fire brigades. This was initially a feature of normal police duty and carried out in ordinary uniform, but specialisation gradually developed in both the staffing and the uniform of police fire fighters.

inally provided only for inspectors and above, was now issued to all ranks.

With many duties rendering helmets impractical and with other organisations beginning to wear police-style uniform, the diced band round the cap, already used by Scottish forces, became the distinguishing mark of the English and Welsh policeman's cap.

Different styles of car coats proliferated in the 1970s and 1980s with 'Gannex' type

A collection of police headgear of the 1980s. (Clockwise from left) Normal-duty cap with diced band; standard helmet; white-topped cap with diced band for traffic officers; beret with badge and diced band for firearms officers. The beret was a compromise between the need to be unrestricted by unnecessary clothing and the requirement for easy identification.

18

Above left: *Police provided the only ambulance service in most areas until the late 1930s. The police driver and crew of a City of London ambulance c.1914 are in full police uniform.*

Above right: *Firefighting was another role expected of police until 1939. Uniforms for this function varied from normal police uniform to the naval-type outfit of these firefighters from Neath, West Glamorgan, c.1926. Tunics and trousers were normal police issue; the seaman's style caps and leather boots make an unusual addition.*

Below: *Kingston upon Hull Police Fire Brigade in 1936 present a much more familiar picture of firemen with large brass helmets.*

Above: *The complete historical range of buttons of the York City police: (from left to right) 1850-1902, brass with simple representation of the city crest; 1902-20s, brass with more ornate crest but no wording; 1920s-1935, a nickel version of the previous button; 1935-53, King's crown, wording restored; 1953-68, chromium, with Queen's crown.*

Above: *(From left to right) Two versions of standardised buttons largely taken into use since 1934; two buttons reissued by Lincolnshire bearing the county crest, demonstrating a return to individuality.*

Above left: *One of the earliest helmet plates (c.1865) used in the Metropolitan Police. It has a Victorian crown with the distinguishing angular shoulders over a laurel wreath enclosing a garter with the force name. The leather centre holds the policeman's divisional letter and his number.*

Above centre: *The ornate City of London helmet plate which takes the form of part of the City coat of arms. Despite calls for standardisation, it has remained unchanged since the formation of the force. The policeman's divisional letter and personal number appear at the base.*

Above right: *Before moves towards standardisation chief constables had freedom to design not only their own uniform but also the badges they wore. This is a version of the Rotherham Borough badge specially created in silver for the Chief Constable's helmet. Since 1945 few if any chief constables have worn helmets, even for ceremonial occasions, and the Mid Wales Chief Constable's cap badge is the standard pattern today.*

Left: *Three colourful lapel badges for special constables when working without proper uniform: (left to right) Scarborough, High Wycombe and Lincolnshire. All embody their authority's crest but the Wycombe badge has a Victorian crown although issued during the Second World War. The other two have King's crowns.*

20

Cap badges: (left to right) small standard badge from Sheffield and Rotherham with Queen's crown and royal cipher; larger ornate Warwickshire badge with King's crown and county crest; a badge with King's crown over George VI cipher from Rochester Borough.

BUTTONS AND BADGES

So many attractive buttons and badges have been created for police forces over the years that a specialist club, the Police Insignia Collectors' Society, exists solely for their study. Insignia on the original uniforms consisted merely of letters and numerals embroidered on the raised collar of the tunics.

The seven prominent buttons securing the front of the coat, with smaller versions later seen on cuffs and rear vents, received varying degrees of treatment by police forces. Plain white metal buttons on the earliest London uniforms were copied by most provincial forces, with pewter increasingly favoured until the middle of the nineteenth century, when nickel became the most popular material used. To emphasise their separate identity from their large neighbour, the City of London, together with a small number of other forces, used brass buttons. The City still uses gold anodised aluminium. Army-style button sticks for cleaning were standard issue in all forces until the advent of chrome in the latter half of the twentieth century.

At various times black buttons have been favoured by some forces. Occasionally produced by painting metal, they were usually made from dyed animal bone and later from synthetic material. Less prominent in the dark, they were often fitted to top coats and also to the early braided tunics of inspectors and above. Forces such as North Yorkshire issued black buttons on all uniform while Leeds issued them only to sergeants between 1895 and 1935.

A few forces continued with plain buttons but the majority, keen to show local pride, decorated them with some identification. One of the first orders placed by forces established after 1840 was for dies to stamp blank buttons. Most depicted local coats of arms but cheaper standardised versions were available bearing a simple crown and the words COUNTY or BOROUGH POLICE.

The 1934 Home Office committee on police uniform ended the variety of button designs. Chromium was arriving, button sticks were becoming obsolete and the committee recommended all police buttons should be standardised with the royal crown and the name of the force. This resulted in some forces using the cheaper alternative of buttons with just the royal crown. Since the 1980s some chief constables, including those of Essex and Lincolnshire, have begun to reissue buttons bearing force crests.

Very few badges appeared on police uniform before the introduction of helmets. The first badge or helmet plate for the Metropolitan force was a laurel wreath enclosing a garter which bore the force name and with a leather centre showing the wearer's number. Many provincial forces copied the design but often inserted the local crest in place of the number. By the 1870s the laurel wreath was disappearing, to be replaced by a Brunswick star.

Badges varied from small and simple to large and intricate. Cap badges were often smaller versions of helmet plates and, while some forces used the smaller version for both cap and helmet, others wore no badges at all. One of the larger badges was that of the City of London. It was taken from the City coat of arms and did not include a royal

crown, despite calls for standardisation; it remains their badge today.

Police badges usually incorporate the crown of the reigning monarch. Collectors classify them as 'Victorian', 'King's' (Edward VII to George VI) and 'Queen's' (Elizabeth II). The correct descriptions are Guelphic, Imperial and Tudor or Edward crowns respectively. A number of forces failed to adhere to the system and the type of crown is not always a reliable indicator of the age of a badge.

As with buttons, the Royal Commission of 1934 urged standardisation of badges and recommended a Brunswick star enclosing the royal cipher surrounded by the force name. They pointed to the disadvantages of easily identifiable insignia, especially when forces aided one another. Communities receiving aid did not take kindly to visiting policemen. Some forces

Left: *Constable Pallister of the East Riding of Yorkshire wearing cap and collar with elaborate scrolled representation of the force initials as badges, about 1930. Unusually, white detachable collars were issued which showed above the tunic and led to the force being nicknamed 'the Vicars'.*

Right: *Four West Riding policemen in 1856 with top hats and knee-length tunics. (Left to right, A sergeant, his three rank chevrons unusually inverted; a senior constable on top rate of pay denoted by two single stripes; a constable confirmed in his appointment, denoted by one stripe, and a recruit.*

Above left: *Sergeant 62 George Matthews, Hastings Borough police (1887-1919), has three silver lace chevrons indicating his rank. The two inverted chevrons indicate he has reached seniority in his rank and is on top rate of pay. His duty armband is worn unusually on the right sleeve, where the two buttons are another unusual feature of his uniform.*

Above right: *Constable 300 of the Gloucestershire police about 1919, wearing a horizontally striped duty armband and a first-aid badge on his left arm. Below the armband are two gold-coloured vertical wound stripes indicating that he was wounded twice in the First World War.*

Right: *A late 1930s night-duty helmet from York on which only the centre of the badge can be easily seen. This centre is detachable for either night duty or when rendering aid to another force. In the latter case it can be replaced by the receiving force's own badge to avoid hostility from the citizens of the town being aided.*

reluctant to change the local identity of the badge, nevertheless arranged for that part of the badge to be detachable.

The original wearing of identification on the raised collars of tunics was continued and when open-necked tunics were introduced it was usually transferred to epaulettes, which had appeared after 1945, or, less frequently, to lapels. Officers' numbers and divisional letters were the most usually shown, sometimes with a local crest.

Above: *Overseas service chevrons were issued to the military after both world wars and the Home Office authorised their appearance on police uniform. Each chevron indicated one year's service abroad. The First World War chevrons (left) were of far coarser material than those issued for the Second World War (second from left) but both were red. There is little evidence that many policemen bothered to wear these. During and after both world wars thin red perpendicular stripes were worn to indicate war wounds. (Third from left) Gold-coloured First World War wound stripe. (Right) Red Second World War wound stripe. Some of the latter were known to have been worn by officers injured during duties in air raids.*

Below: *Standard insignia of police in 1990. (From top) Bath star; large button; crown; small button; chief officers' insignia of crossed tipstaves in a laurel wreath; sergeant's chevrons. Two stars denote an inspector; three stars, a chief inspector; one crown, a superintendent; one crown and one star, a chief superintendent; a wreath, an assistant chief constable or Metropolitan commander; a wreath and star, a deputy chief constable or Metropolitan deputy assistant commissioner; a wreath and crown, a chief constable or Metropolitan assistant commissioner; a wreath, crown and star, Her Majesty's Inspector of Constabulary.*

Other forms of badges and insignia have appeared on police uniform in fairly random fashion. From the late nineteenth century inverted chevrons have been used in some areas to indicate constables' seniority, for example one on confirmation of appointment, a second on reaching top rate of pay. Smaller $1^1/2$ inch (38 mm) red and blue chevrons were allowed after 1918 to indicate years of overseas military service. During both world wars and immediately afterwards thin red perpendicular stripes could be worn on right sleeves to indicate war wounds.

Badges of St John of Jerusalem indicated first-aid efficiency and the Royal Life Saving Society badge showed lifesaving competence. In addition numerous small emblems such as the Yorkshire and Lancashire roses were used to show proficiency. Perhaps the oddest of all insignia is the 'in charge' star awarded since 1920 to officers of constable rank in Gloucestershire who had responsibility for a police station.

24

Truncheons were issued to a motley group of ruffians and criminals by the local police superintendent in Whitby, North Yorkshire, in 1864. It was parliamentary election time and by swearing in troublemakers as special constables and keeping them drilling all day he averted any disorder.

ACCOUTREMENTS

Traditionally four items of equipment are necessary for policemen to perform their duties. They require something which allows them to see and, when necessary, to be seen at night; they need some means of raising the alarm and being heard; they need something with which to restrain prisoners and they need a weapon of defence.

THE WEAPON

While occasionally cutlasses and even less frequently firearms have been used by English policemen, they and generations of their watchman and parish constable predecessors normally had only a truncheon with which to defend themselves. Many police officers complete thirty years service without using their truncheons, but they remain standard issue for every constable.

The word 'truncheon', meaning a short club, has been in the English language since

before the thirteenth century to denote a wooden weapon like a club, and shorter than a staff. However, the word 'staff' is more commonly used than 'truncheon' in police circles today.

By the seventeenth century truncheons were usually decorated with the sovereign's cipher or the local coat of arms. They were sometimes used, like a tipstaff, as a badge of office as much as a weapon. The instruction of the London police ran:

'When called upon to act, and there is any doubt as to their being constables, the police are to draw the truncheon.'

Tipstaves, about 6 inches (150 mm) long, hollow and made of brass or wood, are ancient symbols of authority under the Crown. The crown of the reigning monarch on top could be unscrewed and a document or message placed in the tube. As a token of office the tipstaff became recognised almost like a twentieth-century police officer's warrant card and the ex-

25

An ebony-handled silver-topped tipstaff. It does not unscrew to carry a warrant and would have been a symbol of authority. Some chief constables still retain one as a decorative symbol of their office.

pression 'I'll crown you' is derived from arrests when the policeman would produce his tipstaff and announce 'I crown you'. Mainly used in London, they were issued to Bow Street Runners but Metropolitan superintendents and inspectors supplied their own until 1867, when they became an official issue until finally withdrawn in 1887.

Tipstaves are still represented on the rank badge of chief police officers, which consists of crossed tipstaves surrounded by a laurel wreath.

Early truncheons were usually about 20 inches (510 mm) long and made in hardwoods such as lance, teak and ebony. Extremely hard lignum-vitae, the only wood so dense it sinks in water, was favoured by Inspectors of Constabulary in the second half of the nineteenth century. Decoration continued with the arrival of the new police and varied from force to force. In London the royal coat of arms, MP and the individual's divisional letter and number were normally inscribed.

The long-established Hiatt company of Birmingham produced much police equipment, including many of the best original truncheons, and William Parker of Holborn was a well known nineteenth-century retailer of police accoutrements. Despite such recognised sources of supply, some provincial forces still used local craftsmen to produce truncheons in a variety of different shapes and sizes. In cases of urgency

Some of the many shapes and sizes of truncheons, from a collection in the possession of Thames Valley Police. (Left to right) A Victorian truncheon decorated with royal crown and cipher c.1880. A short parish constable's staff with William IV cipher; shape and size indicate it to be more a symbol of authority than a practical weapon. A heavily ringed grip on the solid West Riding truncheon of the Victorian period. A George IV parish constable's truncheon. A long and slender parish constable's staff of 1823. A nicely decorated special constable's staff issued in the reign of George V. A short-handled extremely heavy George IV truncheon. A truncheon decorated with royal coat of arms and Victorian cipher, with a ringed handle for better grip. A George IV long staff which may have been used by either a parish constable or a watchman.

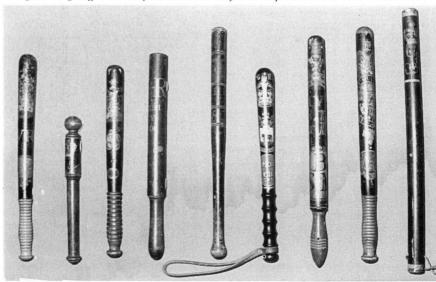

tan force had strict instructions that 'truncheons were not to be used except in dire need'. Despite this there were occasions when situations required their deployment and the first baton charge by the Metropolitan Police was at Coldbath Fields in May 1833.

In the mid nineteenth century the truncheon was shortened from 20 to 17 inches (510 to 430 mm) and, at the same time, the shape began to alter. Instead of being simply cylindrical, the staff became more tapered with a series of rings for gripping the handle. Truncheons were initially carried in tailcoat pockets but when the new

Above: *An unusual record of a section of Kingston upon Hull police parading for night duty at the end of the nineteenth century. With lamps already fixed to belts, on the command 'produce appointments!' the men would present truncheon in one hand and handcuffs in the other for the supervisory officer to ensure they were properly equipped.*

Below: *(Left to right) An Edwardian standard police truncheon simply decorated with the monarch's and the force initials, in this case the North Riding of Yorkshire. A Manchester special constable's truncheon, 1914-19. An East Riding of Yorkshire Victorian truncheon decorated with crown, royal cipher and force initials. A parish constable's staff from 'The Parish of Anthony'. A particularly small (11 inch, 279 mm) truncheon issued to detectives and policewomen for carrying in ordinary pockets and large handbags.*

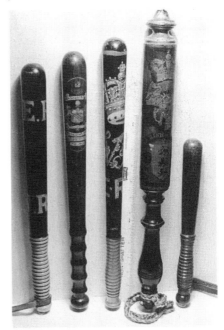

anything handy was used: for example, when industrial trouble occurred at the furniture-making town of High Wycombe in Buckinghamshire special constables were issued with hastily modified chair legs!

In the early nineteenth century, although police invariably used standard-issue truncheons, the local population often armed themselves with a variety of similar weapons, both for defence and often for aggressive use. A Carlisle museum has a fearsome club concealing eight sharpened blades within it. Bludgeons (sticks with a loose weighted head), life preservers (sticks with weighted ends) and flails, or 'swinglers' as they were known, were common. The swingler was described by one contemporary writer as being 'a weapon made like a flail with which they can knock people's brains out'.

Always conscious of the need to restrict the use of truncheons, the early Metropoli-

27

tunic without tails was introduced in London spring truncheon cases were introduced to be carried on the right side of the belt. They were superseded by special sleeves inside the leg of the trousers. Decoration disappeared and in the last decade of the century the Metropolitan Police issued the plain 15$\frac{1}{2}$ inch (390 mm) general-service truncheon with a smaller 13$\frac{1}{2}$ inch (340 mm) variety for plain-clothes men and senior officers. Weighing 14 and 12$\frac{1}{2}$ ounces (397 and 354 grams) respectively, they were made variously of crocus, perpinga or rosewood. This style and material remained fairly constant throughout the twentieth century.

Swords and firearms have never been issued to policemen on a regular basis although some forces routinely issued senior officers with swords well into the twentieth century while 'hangers', short military-style cutlasses, were available for general police use from the earliest days. Mainly kept in store, they were to be used at a superintendent's discretion and were often issued to officers on lonely night patrol, particularly in dockyards.

Some forces did regular cutlass training and dramatic accounts exist of the weapons' effectiveness when used against disorderly crowds. During the 1867-8 Fenian disturbances the chief constable of the East Riding Constabulary drew cutlasses and

The standard modern truncheon, 15$\frac{1}{2}$ inches (394 mm) long, of rosewood and with carved handgrip. This is carried in a long specially made trouser pocket with only the leather thong protruding. When in use, the thong is slipped over the thumb and round the back of the hand to ensure greater security when the truncheon is grasped.

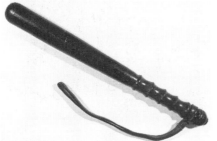

revolvers from Chester Castle but they were locked up with strict instructions that they were only to be used if police stations were attacked.

Firearms have always been available to police but there has always been great reluctance to issue them, except for VIP protection duties.

One of very few photographs of police on duty wearing cutlasses. On this occasion East Riding officers wearing curly-brim helmets are being deployed at a West Yorkshire colliery during a late nineteenth-century railway strike.

MEANS OF RESTRAINT

One of the most serious offences a police officer can commit is to lose a prisoner. Rural policemen, working from their cottages, often without communications or transport, faced great difficulties when they made arrests. Prisoners were regularly kept in policemen's living rooms or bedrooms, often manacled with leg irons to the bed or a convenient chair until they could be 'carted' away.

For detaining someone away from the station, and often with no assistance nearby, a pair of handcuffs has been the traditional answer. Although not completely immobilising a difficult prisoner, they can prevent escape and are small enough to be carried as part of normal accoutrements.

While small firms like Dowler did supply handcuffs, Hiatts of Birmingham were

28

by far the biggest producer and by the early nineteenth century were making the regulation D-shaped metal handcuffs, fastened in the centre by a small chain. A cumbersome key requiring laborious screwing in and out completed the equipment. Many variations subsequently appeared but the D type lasted until the second half of the twentieth century.

Since then 'snap-on' ratchet-type cuffs have come into widespread use and lighter material has replaced the original, very heavy metal.

Many northern forces originally used a style of handcuff known as the figure of eight. One loop snapped on to the prisoner's wrist, the other being held by the escort. With no swivel, a quick twisting of the escort's half was sufficient to bring the most recalcitrant prisoner to order!

Nineteenth-century instructions to police urged discretion in the use of handcuffs and said:

'Handcuffs should not be used except in cases of necessity, when a prisoner is violent and likely to escape ... or the special circumstances render such a precaution necessary to prevent a rescue or the prisoner doing injury to himself .... If hand-

Constable 8 of Beverley Borough holding one end of the handcuff fixed to his prisoner, about 1870. The scene was possibly staged for the photograph, for this is not a safe way to secure a prisoner. The spare cuff should always be locked on to the escort's wrist.

A selection of handcuffs used by police. (From right, clockwise) Heavy-duty figure-of-eight pair probably used in prisons and giving no movement of the wrists. An early pair of D handcuffs, named after their shape, which served for many years until the 1970s as standard police issue; they allow some movement between the hands. A leading handcuff used almost exclusively by northern forces; the smaller loop secures the prisoner's wrist while the escort holds the other loop, which can by being twisted slightly and quickly make the most difficult prisoner quiescent. Modern lightweight snap-on ratchet type.

cuffs are unnecessarily put on, and the prisoner is acquitted, he might bring an action and recover damages against the officer.'

No such restraints on using handcuffs exist in modern times. Provided the minimum necessary force is used to apply them, prisoners are handcuffed whenever appropriate.

RAISING ALARM

Guardians of the law have traditionally operated alone, keeping watch and tackling wrongdoers, often at night and in lonely places. Watchmen and sentries in the earliest settlements had means of warning their fellows and calling for aid: horns were blown, sticks were beaten — anything which made a noise, the louder the better. It attracted attention and frightened intruders.

Bells, often used for signalling alarm, were taken into use by early watchmen, who became known as 'bellmen' in some places.

The origin of the rattle is not clear but an early example in the Police Staff College at Bramshill, Hampshire, indicates that they were first made with a fixed blade and weights which, when swung round, struck the blade causing the familiar snapping sound. Eighteenth- and early nineteenth-century watchmen carried large heavy rattles in their belts. Some were designed to be turned rather than swung and had a small knob fitted on the arm for this purpose. Peel's first policemen were issued with small and usually folding rattles which fitted neatly into specially made pockets in the swallow tails of their coats.

As with truncheons and handcuffs policemen were warned not to use rattles except in justifiable circumstances. Each use of the rattle had to be reported to a senior officer and, if considered appropriate, the offender would be disciplined. Not only could a rattle alert a hostile crowd but Victorian townsfolk were jealous of their sleep and likely to complain if disturbed at night.

Not until the 1880s were experiments carried out in London to find an alternative to the rattle. It was discovered that the sound from a whistle, already being used in some provincial forces like Liverpool could be heard at 1000 yards (900 metres) — almost twice the effective distance of a rattle. The Metropolitan Police issued whistles in 1884, but some forces kept rattles well into the twentieth century. Their withdrawal was not universally popular as the men often found them a useful additional weapon.

The London police whistle was invented by Joseph Hudson of Birmingham in 1884 His first contract for 21,000 whistles was the foundation of a prosperous business Early varieties for constables and sergeants were dull grey 'pea whistles', with a large ring on top and a hard cork ball inside Senior officers' whistles were silvery with an acorn moulded on the top.

The air whistle came into use in the early twentieth century and has remained largely unchanged ever since. Few police officers ever have occasion to use their whistle This is perhaps fortunate for, while officers in urban areas might reasonably expect response to a whistle, those in rural areas knew the sound was unlikely to be heard.

Unlike other police accoutrements, the problem with whistles was not so much the police disturbing the public as the public annoying police. A late nineteenth-century newspaper report drew attention to police whistles being used by citizens to call cabs and by Boy Scouts signalling. 'It will be seen that great annoyance and fatigue is caused to police running about after these indiscriminate calls', the report concluded.

Alternative arrangements peculiar to certain localities are related in the memoirs of a constable from a northern force in the 1920s who wrote: 'When anything unusual happened on your beat, we used to tap the pavement edge with our baton and the next policeman would hear the sound and reply with his baton. It was a very well known sound to all beatmen and someone would answer very quickly.'

Personal radio has revolutionised police communications since the 1970s and some forces have withdrawn the traditional whistles. Others feel they still have a role in drawing public attention in sudden emergencies and that they maintain the traditional appearance of the British policeman.

LAMPS

A policeman's role always assumes increased importance during the hours of darkness, when most citizens are asleep and criminals can operate unseen. The guardian of the law needs to be able to see and, on occasions, be seen at night.

The earliest hand lanterns used candles and were made of wood with panels of cow horn. There is no direct evidence that any of the new police forces were issued with candle lamps although some of the earliest provincial forces may have started with them.

Certainly London police had rape-oil burning lanterns in 1833, as revealed by orders issued on 18th February that year banning the taking of oil from them. Early oil lamps were round and made of black or dark blue lacquered metal. About 7$\frac{1}{2}$ inches (190 mm) high, they had a clip on the back for fastening to the belt and a special leather pad, also fixed to the belt, to prevent staining the tunic and to stop singeing. A thick glass lens, known as a bullseye, focused the dim light and a sliding shutter allowed the light to be concealed if necessary.

Although not powerful, the light from the bullseye was such that a Metropolitan order of 1840 directed that 'Bull's eyes are not to be turned on persons on horseback and in carriages'. The small amount of heat they emitted was appreciated by many night-duty constables.

Oil lamps need regular filling and attention to the wicks. In some forces officers attended to their own lamps and it is recorded that in 1873 the West Riding force granted constables one shilling each month for oil. London, on the other hand, with so many lamps, had a contractor's man to trim the lanterns each afternoon although officers living some way from the station were permitted to take a week's supply of filled oil wells home. For a short time the contractor was stopped and all officers were issued with 'trimming oil cans with spouts and trimming scissors'. In 1871 it is recorded that lanterns, 2183 in total, were again to be 'trimmed by Mr Joyce, the contractor, as formerly. Oil cans and scissors to be returned.'

Not until the First World War did experiments begin with electricity. In 1917 men in Hull were offered one shilling per month if they provided themselves with an electric lamp, which they were required to charge themselves. One hundred 4 volt lamps of the accumulator type were issued experimentally in London in 1919 and leather guards remained on belts to prevent acid burns. In 1920 the remaining oil lamps were withdrawn although some provincial forces retained them much longer.

The introduction of dry batteries allowed smaller and more efficient lamps to be issued. They were still designed for clipping to night belts and usually had a red mask for stopping vehicles. These were common in some forces until the middle to late 1950s. During the following decade they were gradually replaced by torch allowances to individual officers.

31

FURTHER READING

Clark, E. F. *Truncheons — Their Romance and Reality*. Herbert Jenkins, not dated.
Critchley, T. A. *A History of Police in England and Wales 900-1966*. Constable, 1967.
Cunnington, P. *Occupational Costume in England, 11th century to 1914*. Black, 1967.
Dicken, E. R. H. *The History of Truncheons*. A. H. Stockwell, 1952.
Elliott, D. J. *Policing Shropshire 1836-1967*. Brewin Books, 1984.
Hibbert, Christopher. *The English. A Social History 1066-1945*. Grafton, 1987.
Mitton, Mervyn. *The Policeman's Lot*. Quiller Press, 1985.
Ripley, H. *Forces of Great Britain and Ireland — Their Amalgamations and Buttons*. R. Hazell and Company, 1983.
Taylor, M. B., and Wilkinson, V. L. *Badges of Office*. R. Hazell and Company, 1990.
Whitmore, Richard. *Crime and Punishment in Victorian Times*. Batsford, 1978.

PLACES TO VISIT

A large number of forces, in addition to those mentioned below, have museum collection but not all are open to the public and all require prior appointments to visit. Enquiries should be directed to the administration departments of individual force headquarters Many other local museums also have collections of police uniform and equipment.

Greater Manchester Police Museum, Newton Street, Manchester M1 1ES. Telephone 061-855 3290. By appointment only.
Kent County Constabulary, Police Headquarters, Sutton Road, Maidstone, Kent. Tele phone: 0622 65432. By appointment only.
Police Staff College, Bramshill House, Bramshill, near Basingstoke, Hampshire. Tele phone (Librarian): 025126 2931. By appointment only — contact Librarian.
Ripon Prison and Police Museum, 27 St Marygate, Ripon, North Yorkshire. Telephone 0765 3706.
Simms International Police Collection, Winchcombe Museum, Old Town Hall, Winch combe, Gloucestershire GL54 5LJ. Telephone: 0386 602925 or 881111.
South Wales Police Museum, Police Headquarters, Cowbridge Road, Bridgend, Mid Gla morgan CF31 3SU. Telephone: 0656 655555 extension 427. By appointment only.
West Yorkshire Metropolitan Police Museum, The Tyrle, Bradford, West Yorkshire. Tele phone: 0924 375222 extension 22218. By appointment only.
York Castle Museum, Tower Street, York, North Yorkshire YO1 1RY. Telephone: 0904 653611.

A selection of lamp. from the Thames Valley Police Museum: (lef to right) dry battery lamp with re removable disc in fron. for stopping vehicles traditional bullseye oi lamp; an early dry accumulator-type lamp; the Guardian 'Traffic' lamp, an early battery model made in Leicestershire.

Police Uniform and Equipment

Although much has been written on many aspects of the police and policing in England and Wales there is surprisingly little on the development of the policeman's uniform, well known throughout the world, and on the equipment he carries. Beginning with the formation of the first police forces, this book describes the origin and development of the familiar uniform and the buttons and badges used by various forces. The equipment carried by a policeman enables him to defend himself if attacked, restrain his attacker once subdued, call for assistance or raise the alarm, and, if it is dark, see where he is going. While some equipment hardly differs from that issued to the earliest officers, advances in technology have ensured that other aids have changed out of all recognition.

Tony Clarke was a policeman for 34 years before retiring as deputy chief constable of Humberside in 1985. After joining the Shropshire constabulary, he served variously in West Mercia, HM Inspectorate and North Wales, where he was in charge of security for the Investiture of HRH the Prince of Wales. After a secondment to Turkey he went to South Wales, eventually moving to Humberside in 1977. Always interested in history, he attended a course at Hull University after retiring. His interest in police history in particular was aroused by the excellent museum in South Wales and by the wealth of material collected in Humberside from the old constituent forces. He is currently researching the histories of both Hull City and the East Riding forces.

Shire books on textiles, fashion, costume and needlecrafts

Shire Publications Ltd, Cromwell House, Church Street, Princes Risborough, Buckinghamshire HP17 9AJ, UK.

91:1:1

ISBN 0 7478 0126 6

9 780747 801269